Sports Illustrated KIDS

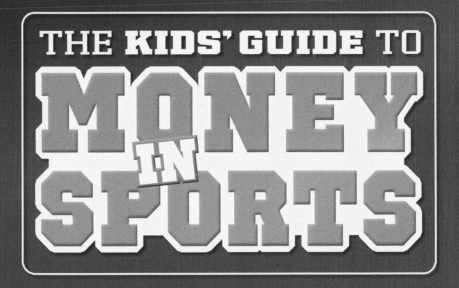
THE KIDS' GUIDE TO MONEY IN SPORTS

BY SUZANNE SLADE

T0052518

CAPSTONE PRESS
a capstone imprint

SI Kids Guide Books are published by
Capstone Press
1710 Roe Crest Drive
North Mankato, Minnesota 56003
www.capstonepub.com

*With gratitude to Ken Mirer, Indiana Football Hall of Fame
inductee, who helped immensely with the research for this project.*

Library of Congress Cataloging-in-Publication Data
Slade, Suzanne.
The kids' guide to money in sports / by Suzanne Slade.
    pages cm.—(Sports illustrated kids. SI kids guide books)
Includes index.
ISBN 978-1-4765-4154-9 (library binding)
ISBN 978-1-4765-5186-9 (paperback)
ISBN 978-1-6663-1498-4 (ebook pdf)
1. Professional sports—Economic aspects. 2. Sports—Economic
aspects. I. Title.
GV716.S52 2014
338.4'7796—dc23   2013032785

Editorial Credits
Anthony Wacholtz, editor; Sarah Bennett, designer; Eric Gohl,
media researcher; Charmaine Whitman, production specialist

Photo Credits
Getty Images: Roger Federer Foundation, 24; Newscom: Cal Sport
Media/Duncan Williams, 31 (top), Cal Sport Media/Larry Clouse,
28, Icon SMI/Chris Williams, 36, MCT/Chris Seward, 40, Reuters/
Shannon Stapleton, 41, UPI Photo Service/Jim Middleton, 22, ZUMA
Press/Gregory Urquiaga, 35; Shutterstock: David W. Leindecker,
42–43, FotograFFF, cover (top), Gary Yim, cover (bottom); *Sports
Illustrated*: Al Tielemans, 7, 11, 29, Bill Frakes, 4, 23, 33, Bob Martin,
9, Bob Rosato, 19, Damian Strohmeyer, 16–17, 21, 34, David E.
Klutho, 25, 31 (bottom), 37, John Biever, 20, 30, John W. McDonough,
8, 27, Peter Read Miller, 32, 38, 45, Robert Beck, 5, 6, 13, 18, 44, Simon
Bruty, 12, 14, 15, 39; Wikipedia: Roberto Coquis, 43 (front)

Design Elements: Shutterstock

TABLE OF CONTENTS

MONEY AND SPORTS

The score was tied at 15 with less than three seconds on the clock. The lacrosse match between the Princeton Tigers and the North Carolina Tar Heels in 2013 was a nail-biter. Then North Carolina took a shot that soared into the net—goal! North Carolina had defeated the mighty Princeton team!

Lacrosse is now one of the fastest growing NCAA sports. At the professional level, the National Lacrosse League (NLL) has nine teams with more possibly on the way. And increased fan interest in lacrosse can mean more **scholarship** dollars for players in college.

Fans can purchase shirts, hats, and novelty items featuring their favorite team's logo.

Whether it's the Olympics, professional sports, or college sports, money is a big part of the game. Athletes pay for their training and expenses. Teams make profits through tickets, food sales, and merchandise. Advertisers pay big bucks for star athletes to promote their products.

As fan support of a sport grows, the money and opportunities surrounding it do too. A loyal fan base is important in all sports. Fans not only cheer on their teams, but they bring in money for the players as well. In many professional and college sports, ticket sales help support teams. But even more important, large crowds attract advertisers who often pay for costly ads in stadiums and arenas.

scholarship—money given to a student to help pay for school

CHAPTER 1

Making It Big

SPORTS SALARIES

Salaries for professional athletes have risen dramatically over the years. Many of the best players make millions each year. Meanwhile, rookie athletes or veterans who are on the decline might earn considerably less.

The highest-earning athlete for 2012 was boxer Floyd Mayweather Jr., who lived up to his nickname "Money." Perhaps even more surprising than his top slot is the fact that he made his colossal $85 million by competing in only two fights.

**Floyd Mayweather Jr. (left)
takes a jab at Miguel Cotto.**

rts stars' salaries don't
up. If players are
en or their performance
ver the years, their
e team drops too.
ball star Allen Iverson
National Basketball
n (NBA) career with the
ia 76ers in 1996.
e number one overall
hat year. His salary
6–97 season was
n. As the young player's
xperience grew, so did
In 2000–01 he earned
n. His salary rose to
n in 2004–05 and to
on in 2008–09.
he aging Iverson started to struggle with injuries
lary dropped. In 2009–10 a torn hamstring
time with the Memphis Grizzlies after only three
finished his season with the 76ers but earned
million that year.

Annual Salaries of Professional Athletes		
Athlete	Sport	Salary
Floyd Mayweather Jr.	Boxing	$85 million
Drew Brees	Football	$40 million
Alex Rodriguez	Baseball	$30 million
Kobe Bryant	Basketball	$27.8 million
Alex Ovechkin	Hockey	$9.5 million
Thierry Henry	Soccer	$5.6 million
Rob Gronkowski	Football	$490,000
Tamika Catchings	Basketball	$105,000
Monica Abbott	Softball	$5,000–$6,000

FAIR PLAY, FAIR PAY?

Women have worked to get the same opportunities in sports as men, but their pay to play those same sports lags far behind. One reason for this uneven pay scale is fan interest. Ticket sales for a Women's National Basketball Association (WNBA) game don't come close to NBA ticket numbers. Along with ticket income, a larger fan base creates advertising and sponsor dollars, which means more money for team salaries.

So what's the difference between men's and women's basketball salaries? In 2012 a WNBA team could spend a maximum of $878,000 for all of its players' salaries. One player's maximum salary was $105,000, while the minimum was $36,570. The maximum salary for an NBA team's combined salaries that same season was $58.04 million. The minimum for a first-year NBA player was $473,604, while a third-season player earned a minimum of $854,389. That's almost the entire payroll for a WNBA team!

Seimone Augustus of the Minnesota Lynx drives the lane against the Los Angeles Sparks.

WNBA center Silvia Fowles played for Spartak Moscow during the off-season in 2009 and 2010.

SALARY CAPS

Most major and minor league sports leagues have **salary caps** so players' compensation doesn't get completely out of hand. Salary caps limit the total amount of money a team can pay in salaries. They also promote fair competition between teams in a league. With salary caps in place, the wealthier professional teams are less likely to "buy" the best players in the league.

When a team goes over its league's salary cap, it may face penalties. One of the most common penalties is a luxury tax. Some teams have chosen to pay the luxury tax to spend more on top players. For example, the New York Yankees purposely went over their $178 million salary cap in 2012. As a result the Yankees had to pay a $19.3 million luxury tax. In Major League Baseball, money from the luxury tax goes to the league. In other sports, the money can be distributed to the other teams.

FACT
A salary floor is the minimum amount a team can spend on its combined players' salaries.

salary cap—the maximum amount a team can spend on its players' salaries

THE NBA CAP

The NBA first started using salary caps in the 1946–47 season. That year the cap for each team was $55,000. Most players earned between $4,000 and $5,000. The NBA cap took one of its biggest leaps after the 1994–95 season when it went from $16 million to $23 million. The jump was due to an increase in revenue from a large television contract with NBC.

NFL Salary Cap History	
Year	Cap
2013	$123 million
2012	$120.6 million
2011	$120.4 million
2010	No cap
2009	$128 million
2008	$116 million
2007	$109 million
2006	$102 million
2005	$85.5 million
2004	$80.6 million

Mark Teixeira (from left), Joe Girardi, Derek Jeter, Ichiro Suzuki, and Robinson Cano of the New York Yankees

PAID TO WIN

Team athletes earn a certain salary over a period of time for their hard work. But individual competitors, such as tennis players and golfers, work differently. They earn money only if they perform well in their sport.

In 2013 tennis star Serena Williams' career prize earnings totaled $45 million—the most career prize money of any female athlete in any sport. She achieved the milestone when she was 31. By 2012 Williams had already earned $38.03 million in prize money. That year she won two first place titles at the Wimbledon tournament in England. She also won the ladies' singles event, earning about $1.8 million. Her first place finish in the ladies' doubles earned an additional $200,000.

Serena Williams

Rory McIlroy

The top finishers in a golf tournament all share a **purse**. Golfers who have the lowest scores earn a larger share of the purse. The winner of the 2012 men's PGA Championship, Rory McIlroy, earned $1.4 million of the $8 million purse. About 70 other golfers won shares of the rest of the prize money.

purse—the total prize money offered to the winners of a sporting contest

ENDORSEMENTS

Danica Patrick

Top athletes earn big salaries and prize money, but they often make even more from **endorsements**. Companies choose athletes who play fair and work hard to represent their products. But if an athlete's performance drops, a sponsor can suddenly pull an endorsement. The same thing can happen if athletes make poor decisions during games or in their personal lives.

NASCAR racer Danica Patrick attracts many sponsors with her skills on the track and her great smile. In 2013 she had 15 sponsors, including GoDaddy, Coca-Cola, Nationwide, and Sega. Her 2012 earnings of $12.9 million—mostly from endorsements—made her the seventh highest-paid NASCAR driver that year.

endorsement—the act of an athlete wearing, promoting, or using a product, usually for money

The Nike "swoosh" logo appears on Roger Federer's headband, shirt, socks, and shoes.

Another top endorsement earner is Swiss tennis player Roger Federer. In 2008 he signed a 10-year deal with Nike that pays about $11.6 million each year. In addition to Nike, he's had long-standing endorsements with Rolex, Wilson, Gillette, and Jura, a Swiss coffee maker company. He's also done commercials for Mercedes Benz. In 2012 Federer earned $71.5 million and about $65 million came from endorsements. That amount made Federer the highest-paid athlete from endorsements that year.

Athletes can continue to endorse brands and products even after they retire. Michael Jordan of the Chicago Bulls enjoyed a long, profitable relationship with Nike. Although Jordan hasn't played ball in years, he still earns tens of millions of dollars each year from his Nike endorsement deal.

A FREE RIDE

Top college athletes don't earn money, but they can get something valuable for their hard work and skills—a free college education. Sometimes they also receive free tutors, special trainers, and one-on-one coaching. Not every sports scholarship covers all costs, such as tuition and room and board, but even a partial scholarship can be a huge help with the high costs of college.

SCHOLARSHIP TIPS

If you're hoping for a sports scholarship, you should start thinking about colleges early. The recruiting process for most students begins July 1 of the summer before their senior year. You could make a video of your game highlights from high school and send the link to college coaches. Don't rule out Division III schools that don't award sports scholarships. Some of the smaller, private schools offer athletes scholarships based on academics.

Harvard-Radcliffe women's
rowing team

2012–2013 College Tuition Rates for Full-Time Undergraduate Students	
Duke University	$43,623
Northwestern University	$43,779*
Penn State	$28,746 (out-of-state)
Purdue University	$28,702 (out-of-state)
Stanford University	$41,787
University of Miami	$39,654
University of Notre Dame	$42,971*

*Includes fees

Many men's and women's sports programs, including tennis, rowing, swimming, gymnastics, and golf, offer scholarships. Sometimes an athlete can gain acceptance into a college that he or she might not have been able to earn on grades alone. College sports provide an opportunity to become a better athlete, which could mean getting drafted by a pro team. College athletes also find other job opportunities in the field of sports after graduation.

CHAPTER 2

The Cost of Being an ATHLETE

GEARING UP

Pro athletes face big expenses, such as training facilities, individual coaching, and travel costs. Specialized equipment, uniforms, and gear can add up too. Some athletes start out by wearing used gear, such as second-hand skates or cleats, or buying used equipment, such as rackets or hockey sticks. But when an athlete wants to compete at the Olympic and professional level, he or she needs the best equipment possible. Sometimes those items have a hefty price tag, such as an Olympic men's skin-tight swimsuit ($395) or a high-tech women's swimsuit that covers her legs ($550). Even a table tennis paddle costs $300 or more for Olympic players.

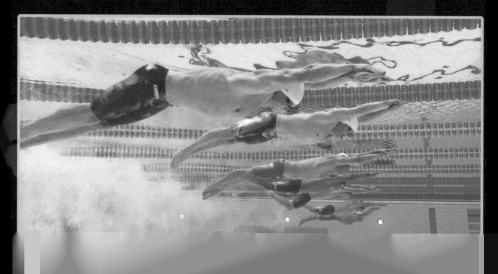

When it comes to gear, hockey is a popular sport that requires lots of equipment to get in the game. The cost of the equipment differs for amateur players and pro athletes.

Hockey Equipment Costs	
Ice skates	$100–$500
Hockey sticks	$30–$300
Helmets	$60–$150
Jerseys	$20–$50
Shoulder pads	$50–$100
Elbow pads	$20–$70
Gloves	$40–$250
Hockey pants	$60–$140
Shin guards	$30–$100
Hockey socks	$10–$30
Mouth guard	$10–$20
Hockey bag	$50–$100

Mats Sundin

SPORTS AGENTS

Athletes may be good at sports, but they aren't always knowledgeable about business **contracts**. Professional athletes usually hire sports agents to **negotiate** their contracts. Many agents have law degrees, so they understand the legal details in contracts. Agents must be firm and professional as they negotiate the best deals for their clients. They also need excellent communication skills as they work to keep both their clients and the sports teams happy.

A sports agent is paid a percentage of an athlete's earnings. The amount varies, but most agents get between 3 percent and 10 percent of a player's contract. Some leagues have rules limiting an agent's cut. For example, an agent for an NFL player can't earn more than 3 percent of the player's contract.

Golfer Martin Kaymer (right) shares his victory with his agent, Johan Elliott.

contract—a legal agreement
negotiate—to bargain or discuss something to come to an agreement

20

Some agents work on their own, while others are part of a sports agency. Agents who work with an agency often provide additional services such as investment advice so athletes will be financially stable when their big salaries disappear.

In 2013 Jay Z formed his own sports agency called Roc Nation Sports.

FACT

Agents also earn money from players' endorsement contracts. Many agents get a higher percentage of endorsement contracts than salary contracts.

Athletes who earn huge salaries often make big purchases. Former basketball superstar Shaquille O'Neal, a big Superman fan, had a round Superman bed that was estimated to have cost $15,000. He also owned a customized sport utility vehicle. The SUV was decked out with leather seats and a Superman logo on the front grill. It was equipped with three TVs and a sound system with six subwoofers.

Former boxing champ Evander Holyfield bought a mansion in Georgia in 1994. The 109-room home had a bowling alley, theater, and 17 bathrooms. The huge estate cost about $1 million a year to maintain. After Evander stopped boxing, he couldn't afford to keep his house. It sold for $7.5 million in 2012, which was only about half of what he still owed on the house.

Boxer Evander Holyfield's former home provided 54,000 square feet (5,017 square meters) of living space.

Brooklyn Nets forward Joe Johnson is crazy about sneakers. His personal sneaker collection totals more than 1,000 pairs. He stores them in a mega-sized closet equipped with a basketball hoop, television, and bed. A fingerprint security system in his huge closet keeps his shoes safe.

Former NFL wide receiver Chad Johnson spent a large chunk of his earnings on fish tanks—two giant aquariums to be exact. One large tank surrounds his bed headboard so he can watch colorful fish swim above his head as he drifts off to sleep. The other aquarium stretches across his entertainment room and holds three TVs.

AN EXPENSIVE EGG

Under extreme pressure to perform their best, some athletes buy expensive items they believe will help them win. Top-ranked tennis star Novak Djokovic, for example, paid $75,000 for a pressurization chamber. The egg-shaped chamber is called a CVAC pod. It compresses a person's muscles at certain intervals and is designed to create the effects of being at a high-pressure altitude. The chamber is supposed to help Novak's body recover after a tiring match so he can play his best the next time he's on the court.

Carolina Panthers wide receiver Steve Smith drives his custom-made Mercedes Benz golf cart.

PAYING IT FORWARD

While some players are known for spending money on extravagant things, many athletes share their money with others. Generous sports figures help those in need by donating money to charities. Some also give their time, appearing at events and helping raise money or increasing awareness for a worthy cause. Some athletes give in more personal ways by visiting sick children in hospitals or by mentoring young kids who need good role models in their lives.

Athletes in many sports have made giving a big part of their sports experience. Tennis champion Roger Federer started his own charitable foundation. His organization helps children in Africa and Switzerland primarily through education and sports programs. Soccer star Mia Hamm started a foundation that raises money and awareness for families in need of a bone marrow or cord blood transplant. It also develops programs for young women in sports.

Tennis star Roger Federer poses with school children from Ethiopia in 2010.

St. Louis Cardinals outfielder Carlos Beltran won the Roberto Clemente Award in 2013 for his charity work.

Speed skater Joey Cheek was in top form at the 2006 Olympic Games. He won a gold medal in the 500-meter event and a silver medal in the 1,000-meter race. He donated the prize winnings from both events—$40,000—to Right to Play. The international organization used his money to help Sudanese war refugees. Cheek's generosity inspired Olympic fans and sponsors to donate an additional $250,000 to Right to Play.

PROTECTING
THE FUTURE

An athlete who finally makes it to the big leagues is set for life, right? Not always. Unexpected injuries can put players out of the game for a few weeks, years, or for good. To help protect their financial future against an unexpected injury or illness, some players take out special **insurance** plans. The cost of an insurance policy depends on the type of coverage needed and the amount. The price of a policy is also affected by the sport the athlete plays, and the age or physical condition of the player.

Many players buy insurance to protect the loss of future earnings because of an injury or long-term disability. Some college athletes take out a policy that will pay if they are injured and become unable to play at the professional level. Athletes with big endorsement deals can buy "loss of endorsement" insurance policies. The plans pay athletes a portion of a canceled endorsement contract if they are dropped by a sponsor.

FACT

A photo of swimmer Michael Phelps smoking marijuana appeared in a British newspaper in 2009. The picture led to the cancellation of his endorsement deal with the cereal maker Kellogg's.

Insurance policies pay out only if the player's particular injury is included in the policy. For example, soccer star David Beckham had $78 million worth of insurance for his legs. When he got an Achilles injury in 2010, the insurance company didn't have to pay. Beckham's policy did not include the Achilles tendon, which connects the heel to the calf muscle.

David Beckham

insurance—protection against loss or damage

GOING FOR THE GOLD

There are no guarantees in sports, and that is especially true in the world's biggest competition—the Olympic Games. Many U.S. athletes dream of winning an Olympic gold medal. But training for the Olympics is expensive. Even if the athlete earns a spot on the U.S. Olympic team and wins a gold medal, will it pay off? Or will the athlete end up in debt when the competition ends?

Coaching and facility costs for Olympic hopefuls depend on the sport. Monthly gym fees for gymnasts run about $1,000. Annual memberships to an **elite** swim club cost $1,500 to $3,000. Training costs for Olympic fencers average about $20,000 per year. Competitive skaters' costs start around $10,000 per year, but that amount rises to $30,000 for high-level skaters.

If athletes make a national team, national organizations often pick up training and travel costs. The United States Olympic Committee (USOC) supports training centers in Colorado Springs, Colorado; Lake Placid, New York; and Chula Vista, California. Each training center provides free room and board and training for invited Olympic competitors. However, the facilities have room for only a limited number of athletes.

The U.S. women's volleyball team plays an exhibition game at the U.S. Olympic Training Center in Colorado Springs.

SACRIFICE PAYS OFF

Gabby Douglas's family made huge sacrifices to pay for her training, competitions, and living away from home to work with her gymnastics coach. Douglas' mom even filed for **bankruptcy** so she could reorganize her debts and keep her home. These sacrifices paid off when Douglas won gold in the all-around individual and team competitions at the 2012 Olympics. The USOC pays $25,000 for each gold medal, so she earned $50,000 for her accomplishments. It's estimated she'll make about $10 million more over several years from endorsements.

Gabby Douglas

elite—describes people who have special advantages or talents

bankruptcy—a condition in which a person is legally declared unable to pay his or her debts

CHAPTER 3

Supporting SPORTS

FANATIC FANS

For avid fans, being at the game for every goal, basket, pass, or check into the boards is important. But being a sidelines spectator isn't cheap. Fans must pay for transportation to the game, parking, and tickets. During the game most people buy food, snacks, and drinks to keep up their energy as they cheer on their favorite team.

Green Bay Packers fans celebrate with Donald Driver after he performs a Lambeau Leap.

Serious fans buy season tickets that guarantee a seat at every home game. Season tickets for most professional sports run hundreds to thousands of dollars. However, season tickets cost less per game than regular tickets. A standing room 2012–13 season ticket for the Detroit Red Wings costs $960 for 24 games, which is $40 per game. The individual game price for the same ticket costs $50.

Tickets to women's games often cost less than tickets to men's games for the same sport. A ticket to a 2013 Chicago Sky (WNBA) game, for example, costs between $13 and $225 for a premium seat. Just across town, a ticket to a men's Chicago Bulls (NBA) game runs $44 to $290.

Some sports leagues offer online subscriptions. The subscriptions allow fans to watch their favorite teams online for a much lower cost than buying a ticket. A single subscription fee allows users to stream live games on their computers, smartphones, or tablets. They also have access to some archived games.

Elena Delle Donne of the Chicago Sky

Derrick Rose of the Chicago Bulls

SPORTS AND ADVERTISING

Fans can enjoy staying at home and watching a game on TV for free, but how are the costs covered? The TV networks pay the sports leagues for the rights to air the games on their network. In turn, advertisers pay TV networks for **commercial airtime** during breaks from the games. Advertisers hope that fans will want to buy the chips, sodas, and other products they see advertised during a game. So in a way, viewers at home are "paying" for free games on TV.

Athletes are paid to represent brands and promote products in commercials.

commercial airtime—an amount of time on television that is purchased to show advertisements

Super Bowl commercials are the most expensive ads on TV. Many advertisers are willing to pay top dollar to reach the more than 100 million fans who watch the game. Super Bowl ads cost more to produce than regular season commercials. These specialized ads often feature famous stars and high-action stunts.

One of the most expensive Super Bowl ads of all time aired in 2011. In a two-minute commercial that cost $12 million to produce, rapper Eminem drove around Detroit, Michigan, in a Chrysler car. Another pricey ad was the 2002 Pepsi ad featuring Britney Spears. Pepsi paid $8.1 million to make the 90-second spot.

Cost to Air a 30-Second Super Bowl Ad	
2013	$4 million
2012	$3.5 million
2011	$3 million
2010	$2.65 million
2009	$3 million
2008	$2.7 million
2007	$2.6 million
2006	$2.5 million
2005	$2.4 million

Brothers and NFL quarterbacks Eli and Peyton Manning film a commercial for DirectTV.

FACT
The 2012 Super Bowl was the most watched television show to date with a record 111.3 million viewers. Thirty seconds of ad time during the game cost an average $3.5 million, which means advertisers spent about 3 cents per viewer.

SPORTS MERCHANDISE

Fans love to show their loyalty by wearing their team's sportswear. Sports enthusiasts often wear jerseys, hats, T-shirts, socks, headbands, and more with their team's logo. The merchandise is sold at games, in major sporting goods stores, and online.

Top 10 Best-Selling NBA Jerseys*	
Player	Team
1. Carmelo Anthony	New York Knicks
2. LeBron James	Miami Heat
3. Kevin Durant	Oklahoma City Thunder
4. Kobe Bryant	Los Angeles Lakers
5. Derrick Rose	Chicago Bulls
6. Deron Williams	Brooklyn Nets
7. Dwyane Wade	Miami Heat
8. Rajon Rondo	Boston Celtics
9. Chris Paul	Los Angeles Clippers
10. Blake Griffin	Los Angeles Clippers

*Chart information based on jersey sales for the 2012-13 NBA season. Source: *Sports Illustrated*

Carmelo Anthony

When it comes to sports merchandise, there's a lot to choose from besides clothing. Fans on the go might like a team backpack, mug, water bottle, or a phone case with a picture of their favorite player. Others might prefer items such as Los Angeles Lakers bed sheets or a Boston Red Sox wall clock. You can get a New York Giants toaster that toasts "NY" into the bread. For those with more to spend, there's a Utah Jazz leather recliner for $1,200 or a Toronto Maple Leafs minifridge for $500.

Sports memorabilia such as bobbleheads are popular with sports fans.

While fans go crazy for sports merchandise, the teams love it too. Big league teams benefit from licensed products because a portion of all sales goes back to them. So buying sports merchandise not only shows team spirit, but it helps the teams as well.

CHAPTER 4

The Business of SPORTS

BALANCING THE BOOKS

For some people, sports are just about playing a game. But sports are also about business. Both individual athletes and teams need to bring in more **revenue** than their **expenditures** in order to survive and compete. For example, a team has to determine the best price to charge for tickets. The tickets must be affordable so people will come to games, but the team also needs to make a profit. If a team can get fans through the doors, it can earn money spent on food, merchandise, and souvenirs.

Fans can buy foam fingers, inflatable bats, and other souvenirs at the ballpark.

expenditure—an amount of money that is spent

revenue—income

Team owners hire financial experts called chief financial officers (CFOs) to manage their money. A CFO helps create a budget of a team's income and expenses. One of a team's biggest expenses is salaries, so a CFO must carefully consider how much players can be paid.

Jonathan Toews

If a team doesn't have enough money to sign a star player, it may pick up a younger player who costs less money. The Chicago Blackhawks drafted center Jonathan Toews in 2006 when he was only 18 years old. Toews earned $850,000 his first season (2007–08). He has become a National Hockey League (NHL) star, and his projected salary for the 2013–14 season is $6.5 million.

TEAM OWNERS

Professional sports teams belong to owners. A team owner buys the team from the previous owner for a certain price. The price depends on many things, such as the location of the team, the team's success, the number of fans, and the owner's personal interest in the team.

Many teams have one owner, but some have several owners. Six people, including former basketball star Magic Johnson, purchased the Los Angeles Dodgers for $2 billion in 2012. That was the most ever paid for a MLB team. Before that record deal, the highest price for a baseball team was $845 million, when the Ricketts family bought the Chicago Cubs in 2009.

Magic Johnson (left)
and Los Angeles Dodgers
outfielder Matt Kemp

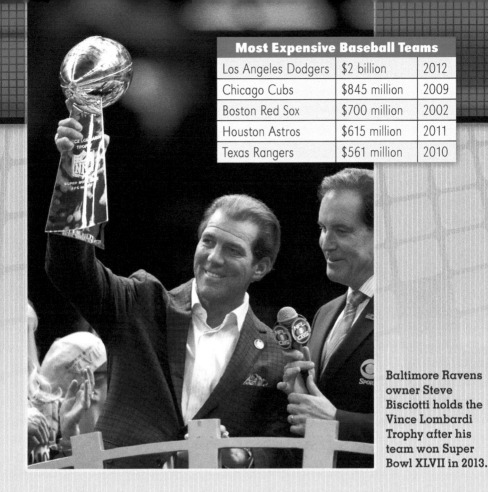

Most Expensive Baseball Teams		
Los Angeles Dodgers	$2 billion	2012
Chicago Cubs	$845 million	2009
Boston Red Sox	$700 million	2002
Houston Astros	$615 million	2011
Texas Rangers	$561 million	2010

Baltimore Ravens owner Steve Bisciotti holds the Vince Lombardi Trophy after his team won Super Bowl XLVII in 2013.

Only one professional sports team doesn't have a traditional owner—the Green Bay Packers. The Packers are publicly owned by fans who bought shares of its **stock**. The team began selling Packers stock in 1923 for $5 per share. It offered stock again in 1935, 1950, 1997, and 2011. So far more than 364,000 people have purchased part of the Green Bay team for a total of more than 5 million shares. Packers stock isn't like regular shares of stock. The shares don't pay **dividends**, they can't be sold, and they may only be given to immediate family members. Fans who buy Packers stock aren't interested in financial dividends. They simply want to support their team.

stock—the value of a company, divided into shares when sold to investors

dividend—a share of the money earned by a business

WE JUST DISAGREE

Professional sports teams can make huge amounts of money, and everyone wants his or her cut. Many players join sports unions so they can use **collective bargaining**. That way they can negotiate with team owners together. Unions often negotiate contract terms such as increased salaries and better benefits.

Fans at a minor league hockey game show their frustration with the 2012–13 NHL lockout.

Sometimes union leaders aren't able to agree with league owners. Before the 2012–13 NHL season, the players' union and team owners disagreed over the players' share of the revenue and other contract details. The argument led to a **lockout**. After 113 days without games, the union and owners finally reached an agreement. Once the lockout was over, NHL teams ended up playing only 48 of the 80 regular season games. Various leagues have had lockouts through the years, with various results.

collective bargaining—a process of negotiations between an employer and a group of employees regarding employment

lockout—a period of time in which owners prevent players from reporting to their teams

Members of the NBA Players Association at a news
conference during the 2011–12 NBA lockout.

League Lockouts

League	Season	Lockout Dates	Result
NHL	2012–13	Sept. 15, 2012, to Jan. 12, 2013	Season shortened to 48 games
NBA	2011–12	July 1, 2011, to Dec. 8, 2011	Season shortened to 66 games
NFL	2011	March 12, 2011, to July 25, 2011	Hall of Fame Game canceled
NHL	2004–05	Sept. 16, 2004, to July 22, 2005	Entire season canceled
NBA	1998–99	July 1, 1998, to Jan. 21, 1999	Season shortened to 50 games
NBA	1996	July 11, 1996	No games canceled
NBA	1995	July 1, 1995, to Sept. 18, 1995	No games canceled
NHL	1994–95	Oct. 1, 1994, to Jan. 13, 1995	Season shortened to 48 games

SKYROCKETING STADIUMS

Sports stadiums and arenas are more expensive than ever before. One reason for the increased cost is technology. State-of-the-art sports venues have advanced security, high-definition cameras, sophisticated sound systems, and huge multimedia scoreboards. A new scoreboard alone can cost tens of millions of dollars. Reliant Stadium in Houston, Texas, paid $15.5 million for two huge scoreboards. The scoreboards, each measuring 277 feet by 52 feet (84 m by 16 m), were purchased in 2012.

Another reason for the rising cost of sports venues is sheer size. Giants Stadium in East Rutherford, New Jersey, for example, opened in 1976 with about 77,000 seats. In 2010 Giants Stadium was torn down. Its replacement, MetLife Stadium, holds 82,555 fans. It cost $1.6 billion to build.

Some venues have a higher price tag because of luxurious extras. The new Yankee Stadium completed in 2009 has 56 private luxury suites, eight party suites, and a members-only restaurant featuring gourmet food. The stadium and all its extras cost $1.3 billion.

FACT

U.S. Cellular agreed to pay the Chicago White Sox $68 million over 23 years to rename their ballpark U.S. Cellular Field in 2003.

FANS COVER THE BILL

The Florida Marlins got a brand new 37,000-seat stadium in 2012 that cost about $650 million. The baseball team paid only $155 million. Team owner Jeffrey Loria worked out a deal with government officials so the rest of the bill was paid with taxpayer money. He hinted that if the Marlins didn't get a new stadium, they'd play ball somewhere else. He also claimed his team didn't have enough money to pay for the stadium.

The *Miami Herald* later reported that the Marlins had made $52 million in profits in 2008 and 2009. That was the most of any team in Major League Baseball. The fans felt betrayed. They were also disappointed by the newly named Miami Marlins' poor 2012 season, the first season in the new stadium. Many fans decided to boycott the 2013 season and not attend any home games. Miami ended the season with the second lowest average for attendance.

OLYMPICS, CELEBRATING SPORTS

The Olympics is a unique experience that brings the world together to celebrate sports. Many cities around the world have hosted the summer or winter Olympics. To be considered as an Olympic host, a city must submit a **bid** to the International Olympic Committee (IOC).

Olympic Host Cities	
Summer 2020	Tokyo, Japan
Winter 2018	Pyeongchang, South Korea
Summer 2016	Rio de Janeiro, Brazil
Winter 2014	Sochi, Russia
Summer 2012	London, England
Winter 2010	Vancouver, Canada
Summer 2008	Beijing, China
Winter 2006	Turin, Italy
Summer 2004	Athens, Greece

Fireworks fill the sky during the opening ceremonies of the 2012 Summer Olympics in London, England.

A bid contains detailed plans of the buildings and outdoor facilities the city would supply for each sporting event. The **budget** explains how much the city expects the Olympics to cost, such as the opening ceremony, buildings, pools, tracks, security equipment, staff, and transportation. The bid also explains how the city plans to pay for the expenses. After reviewing each city's bid, IOC members hold a secret ballot. The city that receives the most votes wins.

FACT

The estimated cost for the city of Sochi, Russia, to host the 2014 Winter Olympic Games is $50 billion.

bid—a written document detailing what a group promises to do if selected for a certain job

budget—an estimate of income and expenses over a period of time

45

GLOSSARY

bankruptcy—a condition in which a person is legally declared unable to pay his or her debts

bid—a written document detailing what a group promises to do if selected for a certain job

budget—an estimate of income and expenses over a period of time

collective bargaining—a process of negotiations between an employer and a group of employees regarding employment

commercial airtime—an amount of time on television that is purchased to show advertisements

contract—a legal agreement

dividend—a share of the money earned by a business

elite—describes people who have special advantages or talents

endorsement—the act of an athlete wearing, promoting, or using a product, often times for money

expenditure—an amount of money that is spent

insurance—protection against loss or damage

lockout—a period of time in which owners prevent players from reporting to their teams; owners do not pay players during a lockout

negotiate—to bargain or discuss something to come to an agreement

purse—the total prize money offered to the winner or winners of a sporting contest

revenue—income

salary cap—the maximum amount a team can spend on its players' salaries

scholarship—money given to a student to help pay for school

stock—the value of a company, divided into shares when sold to investors

READ MORE

Frederick, Shane. *The Technology of Hockey.* Sports Illustrated Kids. North Mankato, Minn.: Capstone Press, 2013.

Hunter, Nick. *Money in Sports.* Chicago: Heinemann Library, 2012.

Slade, Suzanne. *The Technology of Basketball.* Sports Illustrated Kids. North Mankato, Minn.: Capstone Press, 2013.

Sports Illustrated Kids. *Sports Illustrated Kids: The Big Book of Why Sports Edition.* New York: Time Home Entertainment Inc., 2012.

INTERNET SITES

FactHound offers a safe, fun way to find Internet sites related to this book. All of the sites on FactHound have been researched by our staff.

Here's all you do:

Visit *www.facthound.com*

Type in this code: 9781476541549

Super-cool stuff!

Check out projects, games and lots more at **www.capstonekids.com**

INDEX